Owning Your Own Shadow

Also by Robert A. Johnson

He: Understanding Masculine Psychology

She: Understanding Feminine Psychology

*We: Understanding the Psychology of
Romantic Love*

*Inner Work: Using Dreams and Active
Imagination for Personal Growth*

Ecstasy: Understanding the Psychology of Joy

Femininity Lost and Regained

*Transformation: Understanding the Three
Levels of Masculine Consciousness*

OWNING YOUR OWN SHADOW

Understanding the Dark Side of the Psyche

ROBERT A. JOHNSON

HarperSanFrancisco
A Division of HarperCollins*Publishers*

FIRST EDITION

Library of Congress Cataloging-in-Publication Data
Johnson, Robert A., 1921-
    Owning your own shadow : understanding the
    dark side of the psyche / Robert A. Johnson. —
    1st ed.
        p.   cm.
    ISBN 0-06-250422-3 (alk. paper)
    1. Shadow (Psychoanalysis). I. Title.
BF175.5.S55J64 1991
155.2—dc20
                                                90-56468
                                                     CIP

91 92 93 94 95 HAD 10 9 8 7 6 5 4 3 2 1

This edition is printed on acid-free paper that meets the
American National Standards Institute Z39.48
Standard.

Contents

Introduction

I t was said that Dr. Jung's favorite story
went something like this: The water of life,
wishing to make itself known on the face of
the earth, bubbled up in an artesian well and
flowed without effort or limit. People came to
drink of the magic water and were nourished
by it, since it was so clean and pure and
invigorating. But humankind was not content
to leave things in this Edenic state. Gradually
they began to fence the well, charge admis-
sion, claim ownership of the property around
it, make elaborate laws as to who could come
to the well, put locks on the gates. Soon the

well was the property of the powerful and the elite. The water was angry and offended; it stopped flowing and began to bubble up in another place. The people who owned the property around the first well were so engrossed in their power systems and ownership that they did not notice that the water had vanished. They continued selling the nonexistent water, and few people noticed that the true power was gone. But some dissatisfied people searched with great courage and found the new artesian well. Soon that well was under the control of the property owners, and the same fate overtook it. The spring took itself to yet another place—and this has been going on throughout recorded history.

This is a very sad story, and Jung was particularly touched by it, since he saw how a basic truth can be misused and subverted into an egocentric plaything. Science, art, and particularly psychology have suffered from this dark process. But the wonder of the story is that the water is always flowing somewhere and is available to any intelligent person who has the courage to search out the living water in its current form.

Water has often been used as a symbol for the deepest spiritual nourishment of humanity. It is flowing in our time in history, as always, for the well is faithful to its mission; but it flows in some odd places. It has often ceased to flow in the accustomed sites and turned up in some most surprising locations. But, thank God, the water is still there.

In this book we will examine some of the odd places in which the water of life is flowing these days. As always, it is free, and it is fresh, as much the living water as ever before. The main difficulty is that it is to be found where one least expects it. This is the meaning of the biblical phrase "What good could come out of Nazareth?" Nazareth is now holy to us, the birthplace of the Savior; but in biblical times it was the wrong side of the tracks and the least likely place to find an epiphany of the spirit. Many people fail to find their God-given living water because they are not prepared to search in unusual places. It is likely to turn up in Nazareth again—and be as ignored as before.

One such unexpected source is our own shadow, that dumping ground for all those characteristics of our personality that we disown. As we will see later, these disowned parts are extremely valuable and cannot be disregarded. As promised of the living water, our shadow costs nothing and is immediately—and embarrassingly—ever present. To honor and accept one's own shadow is a profound spiritual discipline. It is whole-making and thus holy and the most important experience of a lifetime.

1

The Shadow

The shadow: What is this curious dark element that follows us like a saurian tail and pursues us so relentlessly in our psychological world? What role does it occupy in the modern psyche?

The persona is what we would like to be and how we wish to be seen by the world. It is our psychological clothing and it mediates between our true selves and our environment just as our physical clothing presents an image to those we meet. The ego is what we are and know about consciously. The shadow is that part of us we fail to see or know.*

How the Shadow Originates

We all are born whole and, let us hope, will die whole. But somewhere early on our way, we eat one of the wonderful fruits of the tree of knowledge, things separate into good and evil, and we begin the shadow-making process; we divide our lives. In the cultural process we sort out our God-given characteristics into those that are acceptable to our society and those that have to be put away. This is wonderful and necessary, and there would be no civilized behavior without this sorting out of good and evil. But the refused and unacceptable characteristics do not go away; they only collect in the dark corners of our personality. When they have been hidden long enough, they take on a life of their own—the shadow life. The shadow is that which has not entered adequately into consciousness. It is the

---

*Jung used the term *shadow* in this general sense early in his formulation. Later the term indicated those characteristics of our own sex that have been lost to us. We are using the term in its general meaning in this book.

despised quarter of our being. It often has an energy potential nearly as great as that of our ego. If it accumulates more energy than our ego, it erupts as an overpowering rage or some indiscretion that slips past us; or we have a depression or an accident that seems to have its own purpose. The shadow gone autonomous is a terrible monster in our psychic house.

The civilizing process, which is the brightest achievement of humankind, consists of culling out those characteristics that are dangerous to the smooth functioning of our ideals. Anyone who does not go through this process remains a "primitive" and can have no place in a cultivated society. We all are born whole but somehow the culture demands that we live out only part of our nature and refuse other parts of our inheritance. We divide the self into an ego and a shadow because our culture insists that we behave in a particular manner. This is our legacy from having eaten of the fruit of the tree of knowledge in the Garden of Eden. Culture takes away the simple human in us, but gives us more complex and sophisticated power. One can make a forceful argument that children should not be subjected to this division too soon or they will be robbed of childhood; they should be allowed to remain in the Garden of Eden until they are strong enough to stand the cultural process without being broken by it. This strength comes at different ages for different individuals and it requires a keen eye to know when children are ready to adapt to the collective life of a society.

It is interesting to travel about the world and see which characteristics various cultures affix to the ego and which to the shadow. It becomes clear that culture is an artificially imposed structure, but an absolutely necessary one. We find that in one country we drive on the right side of the road; in another, the left. In the West a man may hold hands with a woman on the street but not with another man; in India he may hold hands with a male friend but not with a woman. In the West one shows respect by wearing shoes in formal or religious places; in the East it a sign of disrespect to wear shoes when one is in a temple or house. If you go into a temple in India with your shoes on you will be put out and told not to come back until you learn some manners. In the Middle East one burps at the end of a meal to show pleasure; in the West this would be very bad manners.

The sorting process is quite arbitrary. Individuality, for instance, is a great virtue in some societies and the greatest sin in others. In the Middle East it is a virtue to be selfless. Students of a great master of painting or poetry will often sign their work with the name of their master rather than their own. In our culture, one brings to his or her own name the highest publicity possible. The clash of these opposing points of view is dangerous as the rapidly expanding communication network of the modern world brings us closer together. The shadow of one culture is a tinderbox of trouble for another.

It is also astonishing to find that some very good characteristics turn up in the shadow. Generally, the ordinary, mundane characteristics are the norm. Anything less than this goes into the shadow. But anything better also goes into the shadow! Some of the pure gold of our personality is relegated to the shadow because it can find no place in that great leveling process that is culture.

Curiously, people resist the noble aspects of their shadow more strenuously than they hide the dark sides. To draw the skeletons out of the closet is relatively easy, but to own the gold in the shadow is terrifying. It is more disrupting to find that you have a profound nobility of character than to find out you are a bum. Of course you are both; but one does not discover these two elements at the same time. The gold is related to our higher calling, and this can be hard to accept at certain stages of life. Ignoring the gold can be as damaging as ignoring the dark side of the psyche, and some people may suffer a severe shock or illness before they learn how to let the gold out. Indeed, this kind of intense experience may be necessary to show us that an important part of us is lying dormant or unused. In tribal cultures, shamans or healers often experience an illness that gives them the insight they need to heal themselves and then bring wisdom to their people. This is often the case for us today. We are still operating with the archetype of the wounded healer who has learned to cure himself and find the gold in his experience.

Wherever we start and whatever culture we spring from, we will arrive at adulthood with a clearly defined ego and shadow, a system of right and wrong, a teeter-totter with two sides.* The religious process consists of restoring the wholeness of the personality. The word religion means to re-relate, to put back together again, to heal the wounds of separation. It is absolutely necessary to engage in the cultural process to redeem ourselves from our animal state; it is equally necessary to accomplish the spiritual task of putting our fractured, alienated world back together again. One must break away from the Garden of Eden but one must also restore the heavenly Jerusalem.

Thus it is clear that we must make a shadow, or there would be no culture; then we must restore the wholeness of the personality that was lost in the cultural ideals, or we will

Ego and *right* are thought to be synonymous in all cultures, while *shadow* and *wrong* are also to be paired. There is great cultural strength in knowing exactly what is right and what is wrong and to ally oneself appropriately. This is cultural "rightness," highly effective but very clumsy. When the Inquisition of the Middle Ages judged someone and often condemned him or her to be burned at the stake, there had to be an unquestioned basis for such a decision. The fact that individuality and the freedom of belief was evolving in the Western psyche added fuel to this one-sided attitude. Fanaticism always indicates unconscious uncertainty not yet registering in consciousness.

live in a state of dividedness that grows more and more painful throughout our evolution. Generally, the first half of life is devoted to the cultural process—gaining one's skills, raising a family, disciplining one's self in a hundred different ways; the second half of life is devoted to restoring the wholeness (making holy) of life. One might complain that this is a senseless round trip except that the wholeness at the end is conscious while it was unconscious and childlike at the beginning. This evolution, though it seems gratuitous, is worth all the pain and suffering that it costs. The only disaster would be getting lost halfway through the process and not finding our completion. Unfortunately, many Westerners are caught in just this difficult place.

Balancing Culture and Shadow

It is useful to think of the personality as a teeter-totter or seesaw. Our acculturation consists of sorting out our God-given characteristics and putting the acceptable ones on the right side of the seesaw and the ones that do not conform on the left. It is an inexorable law that no characteristic can be discarded; it can only be moved to a different point on the seesaw. A cultured person is one who has the desired characteristics visible on the right (the righteous side) and the forbidden ones hidden on the left. All our characteristics must appear somewhere in this inventory. Nothing may be left out.

A terrible law prevails that few people understand and that our culture chooses to ignore almost completely. That is, the seesaw must be balanced if one is to remain in equilibrium. If one indulges characteristics on the right side, they must be balanced by an equal weight on the left side. The reverse is equally true. If this law is broken, then the seesaw flips and we lose our balance. This is how people flip into the opposite of their usual behavior. The alcoholic who suddenly becomes fanatical in his temperance, or the conservative who suddenly throws all caution to the wind, has made such a flip. He has only substituted one side of his seesaw for the other and made no lasting gain.

The seesaw may also break at the fulcrum point if it is too heavily loaded. This is a psychosis or breakdown. Slang terms are exact in describing these experiences. One must keep the balance intact, though this often requires a very great expenditure of energy.

The psyche keeps its equilibrium as accurately as the body balances its temperature, its acid-alkaline ratio, and the many other fine polarities. We take these physical balances for granted but rarely do we recognize their psychological parallels.

A medieval illuminated manuscript gives us this information in vivid form. Here a stylized tree of knowledge, with its golden fruit, rises up from Adam's navel. Adam is looking a little sleepy as if he does not entirely comprehend what he has produced. Two women stand beside the tree. The Virgin Mary is on the left, clothed as a nun, picking fruit from the tree and handing it out to a long line of penitents for their salvation. Eve, naked, stands on the right, picking fruit from the same tree, handing it out to a long line of people for their damnation. Here is vivid commentary on a single tree giving out a dual product. What a strange tree! Whenever we pluck the fruit of creativity from the golden tree our other hand plucks the fruit of destruction. Our resistance to this insight is very high! We would love to have creativity without destruction, but that is not possible.

1. Tree of Life and Death. *Miniature by Berthold Furtmeyer, from Archbishop of Salzburg's missal, 1481. Courtesy of Bayerische Staatsbibliothek, Munich.*

I regret the prevailing attitude at present that goodness or sainthood consists of living as much as possible on the right hand, the good side, of the seesaw. Sainthood has been caricatured as an image of the all-right person, the person who has transferred everything to the perfect side of his personality. Such a condition would be completely unstable and would flip immediately. The balance would be disrupted and life would be impossible.

The fulcrum, or center point, is the whole (holy) place. I agree that we must relate to the outer world with the refined product of the good side, but this can be done only by keeping the left side in balance with the right. We must hide our dark side from society in general, or we will be a bloody bore; but we must never try to hide it from ourself. True sainthood—or personal effectiveness—consists in standing at the center of the seesaw and producing only that which can be counterweighted with its opposite. This is far from the sentimental view of goodness that has been set up as our ideal.

Of course we are going to have a shadow! St. Augustine, in *The City of God*, thundered, "To act is to sin." To create is to destroy at the same moment. We cannot make light without a corresponding darkness. India balances Brahma, the god of creation, with Shiva, the god of destruction, and Vishnu sits in the middle keeping the opposites together. No one can escape the dark side of life, but we can pay out that dark side intelligently. St. Anthony paid for his beatific vision by night horrors—visions of evil parading before him. He bore the tension between these opposites and finally came to that superordinate insight that we can truly call sainthood.

The balance of light and dark is ultimately possible—and bearable. All nature lives in polarity—light and dark, creation and destruction, up and down, male and female.* It is not surprising that we find the same basic laws functioning in our psychological structure. In German there is a term, *döppelganger*, meaning one's mirror image, one's opposite. Goethe was profoundly affected when he approached his home one evening and was met by a vision of his *döppelganger*, the other one who lived in

---

*Our language has lost the ability to speak of the latter in very noble terms. Our philosophy is unbalanced by the very language we use. How do we speak of dark and give it the same dignity and value as light?

❦ OWNING YOUR OWN SHADOW

his personality. Few of us have so vivid an experience of our shadow, but whether we know it or not our psychic twin follows us like a mirror image.

Most people presume that they are the sole master of their house. To acknowledge and then own one's shadow is to admit there are many more sides to us that the world generally does not see. Dr. Jung tells how he first intuited the presence of "another" in his psyche.

> I had a dream which both frightened and encouraged me. It was night in some unknown place, and I was making slow and painful headway against a mighty wind. Dense fog was flying along everywhere. I had my hands cupped around a tiny light which threatened to go out at any moment. Everything depended on my keeping this little light alive. Suddenly I had the feeling that something was coming up behind me. I looked back, and saw a gigantic black figure following me. But at the same moment I was conscious in spite of my terror, that I must keep my little light going through night and wind, regardless of all dangers. When I awoke I realized at once that the figure was my own shadow on the swirling mists, brought into being by the little light I was

16

> carrying. I knew too that this little light
> was my consciousness, the only light I
> have. Though infinitely small and fragile
> in comparison with the powers of dark-
> ness, it is still a light, my only light.[*]

Jung had gone through a highly refined en-
culturating process, from his childhood in a
rigid Swiss Protestant home to the severe discipline of his medical training. Long hours of
concentrated attention gave him a very
focused personality. But this was at the cost
of ignoring the dark and primitive aspects
that appeared in his dream. The more refined
our conscious personality, the more shadow
we have built up on the other side.

This is one of Jung's greatest insights: that
the ego and the shadow come from the same
source and exactly balance each other. To
make light is to make shadow; one cannot
exist without the other.

To own one's own shadow is to reach a
holy place—an inner center—not attainable in
any other way. To fail this is to fail one's own
sainthood and to miss the purpose of life.

---

[*]From C. G. Jung, *Memories, Dreams, and Reflections*, translated by Richard and Clara Winston (New York: Pantheon, 1963), pp. 87–88.

India has three terms describing this place of sainthood: *sat, chit, ananda. Sat* is the existential stuff of life (mostly the left side of the balance); *chit* is the ideal capacity (mostly the right side of the balance); *ananda* is the bliss, joy, ecstasy of enlightenment—the fulcrum of the seesaw. When *sat* and *chit* are paired together, and sufficiently conscious, then *ananda*, the joy of life, is created. This is won by owning one's own shadow.

If we act from the extreme right, we will knowingly or unknowingly have to balance this with some act from the left side. We do not even have to turn our head around to know that we have created an equally dark content. This is why so many artists are often so difficult in their private lives. There is, however, a broader kind of creativity that folds the darkness into the finished product and finds fulfillment in the shadow. This is pure genius. Its attributes are wholeness, health, and holiness. We are also talking about sainthood in the original meaning of the word—a full-blooded embracing of our own humanity, not a one-sided goodness that has no vitality or life.

A friend asked me recently why so many creative people have such a miserable time of it. History abounds with stories of shocking or eccentric behavior among the great. Narrow creativity always brings a narrow shadow with it, while broader talents call up a greater portion of the dark. Schumann, the composer, went mad; the world knows about the very dark side of Picasso's life; and everyone hears stories about local geniuses with their unusual habits. While those with the largest talent seems to suffer most, we all must be aware of how we use our creativity—and of the dark side that accompanies our gifts. To make a work of art, to say something kind, to help others, to beautify the house, to protect the family—all these acts will have an equal weight on the opposite side of the scale and can lead us into sin. We cannot refuse our creativity or stop expressing ourselves in this way; yet we can be aware of this dynamic and make some small but conscious gesture to compensate for it.

Dr. Marie-Louise von Franz and Barbara Hannah, who shared a household in Küsnacht, Switzerland, had the custom of requiring whoever had some especially good fortune to carry out the garbage for the week. This is a simple but powerful act. Symbolically speaking, they were playing out the shadow side of something positive. Dr. Jung often greeted a friend by asking, "Had any terrible successes lately?" because he also was aware of the close proximity of light and darkness.

I remember a weekend when I put up with very difficult guests who stayed days beyond their invitation. I exercised herculean patience and courtesy and sighed in great relief when they left. I thought I had earned something nice by my virtue so went to the nursery to buy something beautiful for my garden. Before I knew what was happening, I picked a fight with the nurseryman and made a miserable spectacle of myself. Since I did not pick up my shadow consciously, I landed it on this poor stranger. Balance was served, but in a clumsy and stupid way.

Many a woman is burdened by paying out the dark side of a creative man; many a man is drained by carrying the dark side of a woman that is the byproduct of her creativity. Worst of all, children often have to carry the dark side of creative parents. It is proverbial that the minister's child will be difficult and the wealthy man's child is in danger of leading a meaningless life.

On top of that, we suffer from our cultural inventions. We live in the most creative century in history, with miracles of technology, ease of travel, and a new freedom from the drudgery of life. Researchers estimate that in an average family household, twenty-eight servants would be needed to accomplish only one part of the work that is taken care of by our mechanical aids. What a wonderful age! But its shadow appears, inevitably, as boredom and loneliness—the exact opposites of the efficient society we have made. On a global level, we have escalated war and political strife to equal our visions of utopia and of a Brave New World. The high creativity of our modern society can be maintained only if we will recognize the shadow that accompanies it and pay out that shadow in an intelligent way.

How, then, can one produce something of beauty or goodness without doing an equal amount of wreckage? It is possible to live one's ideals, do one's best, be courteous, do well at work, and live a decent civilized life if we *ritually* acknowledge this other dimension of reality. The unconscious cannot tell the difference between a "real" act and a symbolic one. This means that we can aspire to beauty and goodness—and pay out that darkness in a symbolic way. This enables us to do the upkeep on the left side of the balance. Biblical custom states that if one can achieve this before sunset or at least before the Sabbath, one can maintain one's inner harmony.

Example: If I do my shadow upkeep after having difficult guests, I will not land my shadow on some unsuspecting stranger. I have to honor my shadow, for it is an integral part of me; but I don't have to push it onto someone else. A five-minute ceremony or acknowledgment of my shadow accumulation after my guests depart will have satisfied it and safeguarded my environment from darkness.

There are times when the shadow also crops up in one's profession. I try very hard to produce the best possible presentation in my lectures and books through discipline and hard work. The whole cultural world would fall if one did not maintain such a discipline. But this instantly constellates the worst in me and activates my shadow. I keep it out of sight as best I can and when it does occasionally show itself I am inordinately embarrassed. Yet I have the devil's own price to pay if I leave the shadow in the unconscious and do nothing intelligent about it. If I do not redress that imbalance quickly, I will soon be rude to someone, turn up a thoroughly nasty side of my character, or fall into a depression. The shadow will claim its dues in some form, intelligent or stupid.

Does this mean that I have to be as destructive as I am creative, as dark as I am light? Yes, but I have some control over how or where I will pay the dark price. I can make a ceremony or ritual soon after doing some creative work and restore my balance in that way. This is best done privately and need not injure my environment nor anyone near me. I can write some blood-and-thunder low-grade short story (I won't have to look far for the characters since the other side of my seesaw has already been set into motion) or do some active imagination,* which will honor the dark side. These symbolic acts serve to balance my life, do no damage, and injure no one. Much of religious ceremony is designed to keep the left-hand side of the balance functioning in a compensatory way.

The Catholic Mass is a masterpiece of balancing our cultural life. If one has the courage to see, the Mass is full of the darkest things:

---

*See my book *Inner Work: Using Dreams and Active Imagination for Personal Growth* (San Francisco: Harper & Row, 1986) for a description of this art.

there is incest, betrayal, rejection, torture, death—and worse. All this leads to revelation but not until the dark side has been portrayed as vividly as possible. If one went to Mass in high consciousness one would tremble at the awfulness of it—and be redeemed by its balancing effect. The Mass lost much of its effectiveness when it was modernized and made to serve the cultural process. One *ought* to be pale with terror at the Mass.*

The central symbol of Christianity, the cross, is a double seesaw with the two axis crossing at the center. It provides the framework for balancing the right and left and also the high and the low. If one can honor this equilibrium and the inclusiveness implied in it, one will be truly catholic (meaning whole or complete). This word needs to be brought out of its sectarian narrowness and given the breadth of its original meaning. Then it will offer a most wonderful revelation.

---

*Since the sublime balancing effect of the Mass is not as effective as it was in earlier times, we rely on less effective ways of balancing today. Horror movies, gangster epics, violence, the fashion for something garish or shocking in our headlines, the popularity of murder mysteries—all of these compensate for our high productivity and creativity. But these are clumsy elements compared to the fine works of art of earlier cultures.

Western Christianity reveals its own imbalance by making one arm of the cross longer than the other. Since we accentuate the spiritual element of reality more than the earthy, feminine, and feeling elements, we unconsciously compensate for this by making the bottom arm of the cross larger than the other three. The Greek and Eastern Orthodox churches know better than this and have equal-armed crosses.

There is an explanation for how our Western cross came to be this way. Christianity was formulated at a time when the earthy, feminine aspects of life occupied a much larger portion of existence than they do now. Most people drew water from a well, walked or rode animals for transportation, plowed the fields, and harvested the crops. They were at the mercy of nature and of their sexuality. Christianity tried to accentuate the lesser-known spiritual aspect of life. This was correct for people living off the land. But our condition is quite the reverse today. We go for weeks without touching our feet to earth, and few city dwellers have anything to do with growing food. When the officials of a New York City dairy discovered that most poor children did not even know where milk came from, they set up a small portable dairy and showed the milking process in the schools.

A theology for modern people also requires a new emphasis. The same basic laws prevail, but we need different ways of moving toward wholeness and balancing ourselves out. The proportions of the cross are equal in an ideal state, but they will vary for each individual depending on the circumstance (the perspective may be different for a man or woman) and the time of life when we examine this subtle relationship. Wherever we find ourselves, we need to honor the part of life that lies in shadow, to redeem those qualities we have forgotten or ignored.

To refuse the dark side of one's nature is to store up or accumulate the darkness; this is later expressed as a black mood, psychosomatic illness, or unconsciously inspired accidents. We are presently dealing with the accumulation of a whole society that has worshiped its light side and refused the dark, and this residue appears as war, economic chaos, strikes, racial intolerance. The front page of any newspaper hurls the collective shadow at us. We must be whole whether we like it or not; the only choice is whether we will incorporate the shadow consciously and with some dignity or do it through some neurotic behavior. George Bernard Shaw said that the only alternative to torture is art. This means we will engage in our creativity (in the ceremonial or symbolic world) or have to face its alternative, brutality.

Any repair of our fractured world must start with individuals who have the insight and courage to own their own shadow. Nothing "out there" will help if the interior projecting mechanism of humankind is operating strongly. The tendency to see one's shadow "out there" in one's neighbor or in another race or culture is the most dangerous aspect of the modern psyche. It has created two devastating wars in this century and threatens the destruction of all the fine achievements of our modern world. We all decry war but collectively we move toward it. It is not the monsters of the world who make such chaos but the collective shadow to which every one of us has contributed. World War II gave us endless examples of shadow projection. One of the most highly civilized nations on earth, Germany, fell into the idiocy of projecting its virulent shadow on the Jewish people. The world had never seen the equal of this kind of destruction and yet we naively think we have overcome it. At the beginning of the 1990s, with the collapse of the Berlin Wall and a new relationship with the Soviet Union, we entered a brief period of euphoria and were convinced that we had left the dark days behind. It seemed nothing less than a miracle that the shadow projection between the United States and the Soviet Union had subsided, after years of the Cold War. Yet here is an example of what human creativity can do: we unconsciously picked up the energy released from this relationship and put the shadow in another place!

Only months later, we were engaged in another struggle, with terrifying technological power behind it. When the United States went to war in the Persian Gulf, once again we saw the rise of primitive psychology—with both sides projecting devils and demons onto their opponents. This kind of behavior, backed up by nuclear arms, is more than the world can bear. Is there a way to prevent these catastrophic wars, which pit shadow against shadow?

Our Western tradition promises that if even a few people find wholeness, the whole world will be saved. God promised that if just one righteous man could be found in Sodom and Gomorrah, those cities would be spared. We can take this out of its historical context and apply it to our own inner city. Shadow work is probably the only way of aiding the outer city—and creating a more balanced world.

A horrible proverb states that every generation must have its war so that young men can taste the blood and chaos of the battlefield. Our armies and navies have a high place in our society and any parade or military band starts hot blood flowing in the veins of men, young and old. Though I consciously question warfare and its place in an intelligent society, I was not immune to that hot blood when I was in Strasbourg one cold evening. I saw a detachment of the French foreign legion marching down the street with their colorful uniforms, their comraderie, and their jaunty song, and I would have given anything to join them. My own shadow had surfaced and for a moment hot blood completely overruled intelligence and thought.

A whole generation can live a modern, civilized life without ever touching much of its shadow nature. Then predictably—twenty years is the alloted time—that unlived shadow will erupt and a war will burst forth that no one wanted but to which everyone—both men and women—has contributed. Apparently, the collective need for shadow expression supersedes the individual determination to contain the dark. And so it happens that an era of disciplined creativity is always followed by an astounding display of annihilation. There are better ways of coping with the shadow, but until they are common knowledge we will continue to have these outbursts in their most destructive form.

Dr. Jung has pointed out that it requires a sophisticated and disciplined society to fight a war as long and complicated as World Wars I and II. He said that primitive people would have tired of their war in a few weeks and gone home. They would not have had a great accumulation of shadow since they live more balanced lives and never venture as far from the center as we do. It was for us civilized people to bring warfare to its high development. And so the greater the civilization, the more intent it is upon its own destruction. God grant that evolution may proceed quickly enough for each of us to pick up our own dark side, combine it with our hard-earned light, and make something better of it all than the opposition of the two. This would be true holiness.

The Shadow in Projection

What happens to the left-hand side of the balance if one does not keep it conscious and give it honorable expression?

Unless we do conscious work on it, the shadow is almost always projected; that is, it is neatly laid on someone or something else so we do not have to take responsibility for it. This is the way things were done five hundred years ago, and most of us are still stuck in this medieval consciousness. The medieval world was based on mutual shadow projection; it thrived on a fortress mentality, armor, walled cities, possession by force, ownership of anything feminine by male prerogative, royal patronage, and city-states in perpetual siege at each other's gates. Medieval society was almost entirely ruled by patriarchal values that are famous for their one-sidedness. Even the Church took part in the shadow politics. Only the individuals whom we call saints (not all of them named or celebrated), the Benedictine monasteries, and some of the esoteric societies avoided the projecting game.

Today, whole businesses are devoted to containing our shadows for us. The movie industry, fashion designs, and novels provide us with easy places to invest our shadow. Newspapers offer us a daily allotment of disasters, crimes, and horrors to feed our shadow nature outwardly when it should be incorporated into each of us as a integral part of his own personality. We are left as less than whole personalities when we invest our own darkness into something outside ourselves. Projection is always easier than assimilation.

It is a dark page in human history when people make others bear their shadow for them. Men lay their shadow upon women, whites upon blacks, Catholics upon Protestants, capitalists upon communists, Muslims upon Hindus. Neighborhoods will make one family the scapegoat and these people will bear the shadow for the entire group. Indeed, every group unconsciously designates one of its members as the black sheep and makes him or her carry the darkness for the community. This has been so from the beginning of culture. Each year, the Aztecs chose a youth and a maiden to carry the shadow and then ritually sacrificed them. The term bogey man has an interesting origin: in old India each community chose a man to be the "bogey." He was to be slaughtered at the end of the year and to take the evil deeds of the community with him. The people were so grateful for this service that until his death the bogey was not required to do any work and could have anything he wanted. He was treated as a representative of the next world. Since he had the power of the collective shadow in him he was supremely powerful and feared. From India through the West we still have the threat "The bogey man will get you if you are not good!" This is how we frighten a child into goodness with the dark side of life.

Our Old Testament has many examples of sacrifice as a device for expelling the shadow (the sins) of a people. It might be argued that ancient and medieval man could cope with his shadow by projecting it onto an enemy. But modern man cannot continue this dangerous process. The evolution of consciousness requires us to integrate the shadow if we are to produce a New Age.

This is an awesome subject, yet the shadow often shows itself in petty and mundane ways. I had a friend whose father was a retired Cambridge professor. The family dog, old and difficult, had to be put in a kennel each winter. Yet when it was brought home again each spring, the whole household brightened. The old man now kicked the dog instead of taking his shadow out on the other family members. It is not uncommon for people to keep a pet to carry their dark side.

Probably the worst damage is done when parents lay their shadow on their children. This is so common that most people have to work very hard to throw off their parent's shadow before they can begin their own adult lives. If a parent lays his shadow on a young child, that splits the personality of the child and sets the ego-shadow warfare into motion. When that child grows up, he will have a large shadow to cope with (more than just the cultural shadow that all of us carry), and he will also have a tendency to put that shadow upon his own children. The Bible tells us that "the sins of a man shall be visited unto the third and fourth generation." If you wish to give your children the best possible gift, the best possible entree into life, remove your shadow from them. To give them a clean heritage, psychologically speaking, is the greatest legacy. And, incidentally, you will go far in your own development by taking your shadow back into your private psychological structure—where it first originated and where it is required for your own wholeness.

Dr. Jung told of a man who came to analysis complaining that he never dreamed. He went on to say that his five-year-old son had the most vivid dreams. Jung took the son's dreams as the unlived shadow of the father and viewed them as part of the man's own psychology. After a month of this, the father began dreaming on his own, and the son's vivid dreaming ceased. By now, Jung's patient had taken up his own burdens, instead of unconsciously leaving them for his child to bear.

My own father took refuge in invalidism and lived very little of his potential. As a result of this, I feel I have two lives to cope with—my own and the unlived life of my father. This is a severe burden, but it can have creative dimensions if I take on this task consciously. Such things are possible only when we are old enough and mature enough to know what we are doing—though we do not usually have this kind of wisdom until we reach middle age.

It is hard to overestimate the amount of suffering that is handed down from generation to generation. Harry Truman had a little sign on his desk while he was president: "The buck stops here." We could give our children the most wonderful blessing if only we would stop passing the buck to them.

I am often asked if it is possible to refuse a shadow projection from another person. But this works only if one has one's own shadow reasonably well in hand. Usually when you receive a shadow projection, your own shadow erupts and warfare is inevitable. When your shadow is like a gasoline can waiting for a match to fall in it, you are fair game for anyone who wants to irritate you. To refuse another's shadow, you don't fight back, but like a good matador you just let the bull go by. I remember a woman who consulted me long ago; her husband had made it his retirement sport to put his shadow on her. She was reduced to tears sometime each day and neither seemed to be able to stop this destruction. I trained the woman to refuse his shadow—neither to fight nor to withdraw into icy solitude but simply to stay grounded in herself. Since she didn't take the bait, the house shook with shadow power for many days. Finally the man saw what he was doing and a conversation of fine quality was possible between them. The shadow returned to its original source and became highly constructive.

There is a wonderful saying attributed to Mahatma Gandhi: "If you follow the old code of justice—an eye for an eye and a tooth for a tooth—you end up with a blind and toothless world." You can refuse a shadow projection and stop the endless cycle of revenge if you have your own shadow under conscious control. To be in the presence of another's shadow and not reply is nothing short of genius. No one has the right to dump his shadow on you, and you have the right to self-protection. Still, we all know how easy—and how very human—it is to have these attacks. At times, the conscious observer in us stands back and says, "There but for the grace of God go I." Jung used to say that we can be grateful for our enemies, for their darkness allows us to escape our own.

Heaping abuse does great damage—not only to others but to us as well, for as we project our shadow we give away an essential ingredient of our own psychology. We need to connect with this dark side for our own development, and we have no business flinging it at others, trying to palm off these awkward and unwanted feelings. The difficulty is that most of us live in an intricate web of shadow exchange that robs both parties of their potential wholeness. The shadow also contains a good deal of energy, and it is the cornerstone of our vitality. A very cultured individual with an equally strong shadow has a great deal of personal power. William Blake spoke about the need to reconcile these two parts of the self. He said we should go to heaven for form and to hell for energy—and marry the two. When we can face our inner heaven and our inner hell, this is the highest form of creativity.

While we generally need to deflect a shadow projection and step back from the slings and arrows others aim at us, there are certain times we can do much good by carrying their shadow consciously. There is a wonderful story about this that shows what happens when we stand back and do nothing—and allow the projection to run its course. A young Japanese girl in a small fishing village became pregnant but was still living in her parent's house. All the villagers pressed her to name the father, to point a finger at the renegade. After many angry words, she finally confessed. "It's the priest," she said. The villagers confronted the priest with this. "Ah so," was all he said.

For months afterward, the people were very down on this simple priest. Then a young man who had been away from the village for some time returned and asked to marry the girl. It turned out he was the father of the child, and the girl had made up an unlikely story to protect him. Then the villagers went to the priest and apologized. "Ah so," he said.

This story shows the power of waiting while others do their shadow work. The priest did the villagers a great service by his silence; by not protesting or denying the situation, he left enough room for the people to work the problem out among themselves. They later had to ask, "Why were we so ready to believe the girl? Why did we side against the priest? How do we face the discomfort and anxiety we feel within ourselves?"

Such things can only be accomplished if our own shadow is reasonably well in hand and we are not tempted to plan our own retaliation.

We must remember how easy it is to give a gift and then spoil it with some shadow quality that is lurking in the background.

We are advised to love our enemies, but this is not possible when the inner enemy, our own shadow, is waiting to pounce and make the most of an incendiary situation. If we can learn to love the inner enemy, then there is a chance of loving—and redeeming—the outer one.

Goethe's *Faust*, perhaps the greatest example in literature of the meeting of ego and shadow, is about a pale, dried-up professor who has come to the point of suicide because of the unlivable distance between his ego and his shadow—his seesaw has been burdened to the breaking point. At this point Faust meets his equally impossible shadow, Mephistopheles, who appears as his lordship, the devil. The explosion of energy at the meeting is extreme. Yet they persevere and their long, vivid story is our best instruction in the redemption of ego and shadow. Faust is saved from his lifelessness and becomes a red-blooded person capable of passion; Mephistopheles is saved from his amoral life and also discovers his capacity to love. *Love* is the one word in our

Western tradition adequate to describe this synthesis of ego and shadow.* *Faust* shows with great power that the redemption of the ego is possible only as the redemption of the shadow parallels it. As the shadow is drawn up into consciousness, it becomes softer, more pliable, more gentle. Faust's character is filled out by the addition of his shadow. He is made whole by his encounter with Mephistopheles, and the same is true in reverse. Better said, neither ego nor shadow can be redeemed unless its twin is transformed.

It is this rubbing together that brings them both back to their original wholeness. This is nothing less than healing the split between heaven and hell. Lucifer (another name for our shadow) was once part of the heavenly host, and he must be restored to his rightful place by the end of time. This vast mythological statement applies to the individual psyche as well: it tells us that it is the task of every man and woman to restore the shadow and redeem our rejected qualities.

---

*See my book *Transformation: Understanding the Three Levels of Masculine Consciousness* (San Francisco: Harper-Collins, 1991) for a detailed study of this great drama.

The Gold in the Shadow

I have written of the shadow as the dark, unacceptable part of oneself. But I also have noted that it is possible to project from the shadow the very best of oneself onto another person or situation. Our hero-worshiping capacity is pure shadow; in this case our finest qualities are refused and laid on another. It is hard to understand, but we often refuse to bear our noble traits and instead find a shadow substitute for them. A fourteen-year-old boy hero-worships a sixteen year old and asks him to carry what the fourteen year old is not yet capable of doing; in a few months he has assimilated that capacity and is living what he relegated to shadow only shortly before. Probably an eighteen year old then is his hero that he soon catches up with. Development generally takes this means of introducing the next stage of its progress. Today's hero is tomorrow's character.

Early in my analysis I had a startling dream in which I ate Albert Schweitzer, a hero of mine at the time. If one can reduce the exaggerated quality of the dream, it was saying that I must accept a Schweitzer-like quality of my own and stop projecting it onto an outer hero. Of course it is a matter of degree, but the dream was correct in saying that I had to become an Albert Schweitzer. All heroes need internalizing. Of course, the childish part of me resisted this development with all its power.

At the time I wondered, "How is it possible to live out so many aspects of the human personality?" Schweitzer had doctorates in music, medicine, and philosophy and was a great humanitarian. He was clearly a Renaissance man. Yet I could not let him carry my own potential; it was up to me to follow my own interests—music, psychology, and healing—and combine them to the best of my abilities.

It is very puzzling to examine our capacity for projecting our best qualities. It is as if we fear that heaven might come too soon! From the point of view of our ego, the appearance of a sublime trait might upset our whole personality structure. T. S. Eliot described this most forcefully in his play *Murder in the Cathedral:*

> Forgive us, O Lord, we acknowledge
> ourselves as type of the
>   common man,
> Of the men and women who shut the door
> and sit by the fire;

> Who fear the blessings of God, the
> loneliness of the night of God,
>   the surrender required, the depriva-
> tion inflicted;
> Who fear the injustice of men less than
> the justice of God;
> Who fear the hand at the window, the fire
> in the thatch, the fist in
>   the tavern, the push into the canal,
> Less than we fear the love of God.*

My good friend Jack Sanford, a Jungian analyst and Episcopal priest in San Diego, was giving one of his finely crafted lectures and, in his usual careful style, made this startling comment: "You must understand, God loves your shadow much more than he does your ego!" I expected a thunderbolt from the skies or at least large objections from the audience. No word from anyone; but a later conversation with him brought elaboration of his comment:

> The ego is . . . primarily engaged in its
> own defense and the furtherance of its
> own ambitions. Everything that interferes
> with it must be repressed. The [repressed]
> elements . . . become the shadow. Often

---

*T. S. Eliot, *Murder in the Cathedral,* in *The Complete Poems and Plays: 1909–1950* (New York: Harcourt Brace, 1971), p. 221.

these are basically positive qualities.

There are, in my view, two "shadows": (1) the dark side of the ego, which is carefully hidden from itself and which the ego will not acknowledge unless forced to by life's difficulties, and (2) that which has been repressed in us lest it interfere with our egocentricity and, however devilish it may seem, is basically connected to the Self.

In a showdown God (Self) favors the shadow over the ego, for the shadow, with all of its dangerousness, is closer to the center and more genuine.*

We live in an age barely ready to hear this reappraisal of the light and dark sides of human nature. But we must hear if we are to escape conflict that probably would destroy the whole of civilization. We can no longer afford to put our own unlived side out on someone else.

Jung warned us that it would not be too difficult to get the skeletons out of the closet from a patient in analysis but it would be exceedingly difficult to get the gold out of the shadow. People are as frightened of their capacity for nobility as of their darkest sides.

---

*See John Sanford's excellent book *The Strange Trial of Dr. Hyde* (San Francisco: Harper & Row, 1987) for an elaboration of this theme.

If you find the gold in someone he will resist it to the last ounce of his strength. This is why we indulge in hero-worship so often. It is much easier to admire a Dr. Schweitzer from afar than to be my own (lesser) version of those qualities.

I have almost a sixth sense of the gold in another person and I delight in acquainting others with their high worth and value. More often than not they will resist that process with all their energy. Or they may put that value on me instead of recognizing it as their own—as effective an evasion as refusing the quality. Beauty (or worth) is in the eyes of the beholder.

So much energy lies wrapped up in the shadow. If we have exploited the ego and worn out our known capacities, our unused shadow can give us a wonderful new lease on life.

Two things go wrong if we project our shadow: First, we do damage to another by burdening him with our darkness—or light, for it is as heavy a burden to make someone play hero for us. Second, we sterilize ourselves by casting off our shadow. We then lose a chance to change and miss the fulcrum point, the ecstatic dimension of our own lives.

A wise woman once showed me how to get more energy when I complained that I was exhausted before lecturing. She instructed me to go to a private room just before the talk, take a towel, dampen it so it would be very heavy, then throw the towel, wrapped up into a ball, at the floor as hard as I could—and shout. I felt infinitely foolish doing this, for it is not my style. But when I walked out to the lecture platform after such an exercise there was fire in my eyes. I had energy and stamina and voice. I did a courteous, well-structured lecture. The shadow backed me but did not overwhelm me.

If you can touch your shadow—within form—and do something out of your ordinary pattern, a great deal of energy will flow from it. There is a curious fact based on this dynamic. Parrots learn profanity more easily than common phrases since we utter our curses with so much vigor. The parrot doesn't know the meaning of these words, but he hears the energy invested in them. Even animals can pick up on the power we have hidden in the shadow!

The Shadow in Middle Age

In middle age one gets tired of the involuntary round trips between the two ends of the seesaw. It slowly dawns on us, if we are alert, that the middle ground is the best. To our surprise, that middle ground is not the gray compromise that we feared but the place of ecstasy and joy. The great visions of the religious world—such as we find in the Book of Revelation—are based on a sublime sense of symmetry and balance. They give us a picture of that middle place that is the product of honoring both extremes. Ancient China called this the Tao and said the middle way is not a compromise but a creative synthesis.

One cannot stay very long in this middle place, for it is a knife-edge, outside space and time. A moment of it is enough to give meaning to long stretches of ordinary life. India warns that if one touches that place for more than a short time one will lose one's orientation and die. There is small danger of this to most of us, however.

Better suited to our Western life is the concept of standing in the middle of the teeter-totter with two feet planted so we can balance easily. This honors the duality but keeps both elements within reach. Each tempers the and no serious split occurs. This is not a gray compromise but a strong and balanced life.

The early part of adulthood is devoted almost entirely to discipline. One prepares for a profession, learns the social graces, cultivates a marriage, and improves one's earning capacity—and all of these activities invariably create a large shadow. There are elements we had to leave behind, elements that had to be "unchosen" in order to produce a cultured life. By middle age, the cultural process is mostly complete—and very dry. It is as if we have wrung all the energy out of our character and at this point, the energy of the shadow is very great. We are suddenly subject to explosions that have the power to overturn the product we have worked so hard to create. We may fall in love, break up a marriage, storm out of a job in desperation as we try to relieve ourselves of this monotony. These are extremely dangerous moments, but they can set the stage for a whole new phase of life, if we learn how to take the energy of the shadow and use it correctly.

I once had as a patient an artist who drew eyebrows on the thousands of celluloid pictures that make up an animated cartoon. He was so good at making expressive eyebrows that he did nothing else; this went on day after day, year after year, until one day he looked up from his desk, swore, and walked out. He came into my consulting room with this middle-age crisis, having worn out a specialization that had served him very well. I told him he had totally exhausted that part of his life and would have to contact the unlived shadow if he wished to find a new vitality. Being a very nice person, he had a hard time making that contact. His involuntary swearing had been a good start. Correctly handled, this would lead to a new source of creativity and give him a new lease on life. Stupidly handled, it would lead only to destruction, and to the loss of form and structure. Heaven and skid row are separated only by an act of consciousness.

An early edition of *Psychology Today* had a very fine article advising us to change professions at age fifty. The author described the worn-out feeling that most people experience when their profession has reached its apex and there is little more to learn from it. He went on boldly to suggest that we take one or two years off and retrain in an entirely new career. The navy admiral might become a minister and the film developer might become a salesman.

In Eastern Europe there is a system of teaching languages to adults that also taps this energy to good advantage and calls upon the unlived life. In this concentrated course of study, one chooses an identity completely opposite from one's actual life. The college professor might present himself as a pirate, the conman as a priest. The most astonishing eruptions of energy occur in this way! That energy aids in the assimilation of a new language—a task that might be just another drudgery if done from one's ordinary personality.

The Ceremonial World

I have mentioned there are ritual ways of approaching the shadow and having a creative relationship with it. Yet, how does one make such a ceremony? First you must have the contents of both your ego and your shadow in your two hands—a difficult task to accomplish! No one can do anything with a part of one's nature one does not know anything about. Medieval heroes had to slay their dragons; modern heroes have to take their dragons back home to integrate into their own personality.

In this ritual you must find one of the left-hand contents of your personality and give it expression in some way that satisfies it but does not do damage to anything in the right-hand personality. You can draw it, sculpt it, write a vivid story about it, dance it, burn something, or bury it—anything that gives expression to that material without doing damage. As we've said, the most terrible things go on ceremonially in the Mass, but the altar rail is a container, and the priest, who is almost inhumanly close to the drama, is robed to protect himself from the too-great power of the event. He also does his rituals in the sacristy before and after the Mass, to protect himself from the superhuman force he has invoked. Remember, a symbolic or ceremonial experience is real and affects one as much as an actual event.

The psyche is unaware of the difference between an outer act and an interior one. Our shadow qualities are lived out equally well—from the viewpoint of Self—either way. Culture can only function if we live out the unwanted elements symbolically. All healthy societies have a rich ceremonial life. Less healthy ones rely on unconscious expressions: war, violence, psychosomatic illness, neurotic suffering, and accidents are very low-grade ways of living out the shadow. Ceremony and ritual are a far more intelligent means of accomplishing the same thing.

Ceremonies the world over, and from every age, consist mostly of destruction: sacrifice, burning, ritual killing, bloodletting, fasting, and sexual abstention. Why? These are the ritual languages that safeguard the culture by paying out the shadow in a symbolic way. It is easy to fall into the error of thinking that we protect the culture by obliterating the destructive elements. But we will see that there is no way to energize a culture except by an incorporation of them. That is why a true religious ceremony has to contain as much darkness as light. Again, look at the Catholic Mass and you will see a perfect balance of destruction and creation, of evil and redemption.

All of this flies very much in the face of traditional thinking. Our present model seems to be that if we can do something sufficiently creative, that will overwhelm the dark forces and we will have triumphed. But a very different solution is required.

The creative act acknowledges the whole of reality. It is not a partial response. Our penchant for the light blinds us to the greater reality and keeps us from this larger vision. Reality (and if this is not God I have no idea of what is) is not found in any single view of life, no matter how attractive that view may be, but in the wholeness of our own experience.

We find a particularly touching example of an attempt to incorporate the shadow in the story of Marie Antoinette. The queen was bored with life in the most ostentatious palace in the world. One day she decided she wanted to touch something of the earth and ordered barns built on the palace grounds where she would keep some cows. She would be a milkmaid! The best architects of France were employed, the stables were built (they can still be seen at Versailles, where they are treasured for their beauty), and fine milk cows were imported from Switzerland. On the day when everything was ready, the queen prepared to sit on a three-legged stool and begin her career as a milkmaid. Yet at the last moment she found this distasteful and ordered her servants to do the milking.

The queen's original impulse was correct:

she needed something to balance the formality of her court. If she had continued her ceremony of milking, her life—and the history of France—might have taken a different turn. Instead, she was beheaded. The earthy side of the court emerged in this brutal act when it might have been lived out in the simple gestures of a milkmaid.

Marie Antoinette rightly tried to balance her highly refined life with some peasant task. But she failed to see things through and was repelled by the literal act of milking. If she had found some way of honoring this earthy impulse and keeping the refinement of the court, this would have been sheer genius. Who knows how many outwardly destructive things might be averted if we gave voice to the shadow in a ceremonial way?

Our fate can truly be altered if we have the courage to embrace the opposites. In this case, milking was the gold in the shadow—the saving grace. While most rituals center on the dark side of the personality, it is important to remember that golden opportunities also come from the same source. And they can resist our efforts to incorporate them even more than the dark elements!

This ideal of balance is illustrated to us every day of our American lives but rarely noticed. Observe a U.S. dollar bill, which is often in our hands. There is a pyramid with an eye at the apex. The bottom of the triangle represents the duality of our perception. On the ego-shadow axis, we see the pairs of opposites: right and wrong, good and evil, light and dark. As long as we concern ourselves with this scale the best we can hope for is an endless contradiction. But if our consciousness is sufficient, we can synthesize these warring elements and come to the all-knowing eye at the central point. On the dollar bill, the eye is raised above the opposites to indicate its superior position.

Light from this central place has no opposite. Like the Grail Castle, it is outside time and space.* And we find it in a moment of transcendence. In a flash, what looked like a gray compromise becomes a synthesis of dazzling brilliance. Our own Scripture tells us, "If thy eye be single, thy whole body shall be filled with light" (Matt. 6:22). The singleness of

---

* See my book *He: Understanding Masculine Psychology,* revised edition (New York: Harper & Row, 1989) for a description of the Grail Castle.

the eye, the center of the seesaw, is the place of enlightenment. This represents a whole new order of consciousness; the inscription on the dollar bill—"Novus Ordo Seclorum"—promises that new age.

2

Romantic Love as Shadow

It comes as a great surprise to discover that the most powerful and valuable projection one ever makes is in falling in love. This too is a shadow projection and probably the most profound religious experience one is ever likely to have. Please remember that the shadow, in Jung's early usage, was anything that lay in the unconscious part of one's personality. Also remember that this discussion is about falling in love, not the act of loving.

To fall in love is to project the most noble and infinitely valuable part of one's being onto another human being, though sometimes under rare circumstances it may be projected

61

onto something other than a human. There are people who put their divine capacity on a profession or art or even a place. Language is accurate in saying that such a person has fallen in love with medicine, the works of Picasso, or the Ojai Valley. Most of our examples, however, will be drawn from the experience of seeing our own image of divinity in another human being. To make this examination all the more difficult, we have to say that the divinity we see in others is truly there, but we don't have the right to see it until we have taken away our own projections. How difficult! How can one say that the projection is not true but that the divinity of one's beloved is? Making this fine differentiation is the most delicate and difficult task in life.

Romantic love, or falling in love, is different from loving, which is always a quieter and more humanly proportioned experience. There is always something overblown and bigger-than-life about falling in love.

Projecting Our God Image

To fall in love is to project that particularly golden part of one's shadow, the image of God—whether masculine or feminine—onto another person. Instantly, that person is the carrier of everything sublime and holy. One waxes eloquent in praise of the beloved and uses the language of divinity. But this experience is from the extreme right-hand side of the seesaw and invariably constellates its opposite. When in-loveness turns into its opposite, there is nothing more bitter in human experience. Most marriages in the West begin with a projection, go through a period of disillusionment, and, God willing, become more human. That is to say, they come to be based on the profound reality that is the other person. While in-loveness is close proximity to God, love based on reality serves our humble condition far better.

Though no one notices at the time, in-loveness obliterates the humanity of the beloved. One does a curious kind of insult to another by falling in love with him, for we are really looking at our own projection of God, not at the other person. If two people are in love, they tread on star dust for a time and live happily ever after—that is so long as this experience of divinity has obliterated time for them. Only when they come down to earth do they have to look at each other realistically and only then does the possibility of mature love exist. If one person is in love and the other not, the cooler one is likely to say, "We would have something better between us if you would look at me rather than at your image of me."

A James Thurber cartoon sums up the stage of disillusionment: A middle-aged husband and wife confront one another with the words, "Well, who took the magic out of it?" True, when the projection of in-loveness is exhausted, the other side of reality—and the very dark possibilities in human exchange—take over. If we can survive this, then we have human love—far less exciting than divine love, but far more stable.

The shadow is very important in marriage, and we can make or break a relationship depending on how conscious we are of this. We forget that in falling in love, we must also come to terms with what we find annoying and distasteful—even downright intolerable—in the other and also in ourselves. Yet it is precisely this confrontation that leads to our greatest growth.

I recently heard about a couple who had the good sense to call upon the shadow in a prewedding ceremony. The night before their marriage, they held a ritual where they made their "shadow vows." The groom said, "I will give you an identity and make the world see you as an extension of myself." The bride replied, "I will be compliant and sweet, but underneath I will have the real control. If anything goes wrong, I will take your money and your house." They then drank champagne and laughed heartily at their foibles, knowing that in the course of the marriage, these shadow figures would inevitably come out. They were ahead of the game because they had recognized the shadow and unmasked it.

When we project our God image on our mates, that is just as dangerous as projecting our darkness, fear, and anxiety. We say to the beloved, "I expect you to give me divine inspiration, to be the sole source of my creativity. I give you the power to transform my life." In this way, we ask the beloved to do what our spiritual disciplines have done in the past: make us new, redeem us, save our souls.

Something extraordinary happened in the twelfth century when the age of romanticism sprang up out of the Western collective unconscious and we discovered the art of seeing the godhead in another human being. This was known much earlier in the Eastern world, but confined to the relationship between a guru and his student. Aware of the great power of this experience, the Eastern world kept it in the narrow confines of the religious life and forbade it in ordinary relationships. It is wise to put such a force in a container large enough to bear it. Ordinary human relations where we play out this divine drama are not of this magnitude.

The faculty of in-loveness, romantic love, is relatively recent in our history. With it, Western humanity has loosed the most sublime feeling we are capable of and set ourselves up for the greatest suffering we will ever know. Nearly every modern novel addresses our powerful motivation to fall in love—or the anguish of broken or unrequited love. For better or for worse, modern humanity has the power of romance. At best, it is the highest faculty of the human race; at worst, it is probably the most painful experience known to us. The winds that were sown in the twelfth century are the whirlwinds of the twentieth.

We are the inheritors of two myths that surfaced in the twelfth century. The grail myth speaks about the relationship of individuality and the spiritual quest; the myth of Tristan and Iseult introduces us to the power of romantic love. Both suggest a new capacity for direct experience of God. Whether this highly charged experience can be assimilated still remains to be seen. Before these two great myths, Western humanity had always honored the greatness of God in a collective container. God resided in the tabernacle of the Church and did not touch one's personal life very directly. One worshiped in terms of the microcosm, making gestures befitting one's own small stature. This is safety, sanity, ritual. This is still so in all other cultures to this day. Yet in the twelfth century, we entertained the incredible possibility of touching the high voltage of God in a personal way. In these two myths, humankind said, "Moses may have been forbidden to see God directly but I will!" To understand these two myths is to understand the modern dilemma. A true myth gives a pulse reading of a whole culture, a valuable insight into its character and destiny.*

Tristan and Iseult give us one outcome of romantic love. They show us the pitfalls of

---

* See *He* for a discussion of the grail myth and *We: Understanding the Psychology of Romantic Love* (San Francisco: Harper & Row, 1983) for a discussion of romantic love.

projecting our divinity upon another human being. In terrifying starkness, we see the chaos that ensues when we try to mix these levels. It is something like connecting the house wiring to a 10,000-volt power line. Nothing of the ordinary 110-volt structure can stand this overload. Attractive as the idea of 10,000 volts is, it can be maintained only within a container commensurate with its power. No ordinary human container can ever survive the impact of 10,000 volts. Yet our culture prescribes this 10,000-volt experience as the basis for every marriage. When marriages survive, it is because both partners have moved down to the 110-volt human level and learned the art of loving.

The 110-volt love is much more valuable and humanly assimilable than the extravagant pyrotechnics of the 10,000-volt display. Love, in its human proportions, is far more valuable than the leap-into-the-heavens experience of romance.

The Personal Experience of Romanticism

The story of Tristan and Iseult tells of two lovers who ripped off the protecting veil of custom and were swept away into a level of reality that neither could sustain. They accidentally drank the love potion that had been reserved for the king and queen and took into themselves a divine power that was too much for them to handle. Few people have survived this experience since. At best, we've gained a new faculty that we may grow into—given enough time; at worst, it may be the unforgivable sin to take into our own power something that is so large and so impersonal in character. At any rate, we now have touch with 10,000 volts of energy and are doing very badly with it.

It is not likely that humankind will relinquish this terrible power, and I am not sure it could be put back where it came from if we would. We modern people find ourselves in the dilemma of having taken a power we cannot stand but that we cannot relinquish.

The myth of Tristan and Iseult is played out again by every couple in love, yet we have a chance to contribute to its evolution by making a conscious art of relationship. If one could see the splendor of God—in both its light and dark aspects—this experience would not have to end in disillusionment and bitterness.

After many centuries, the vision of God incarnate has suddenly become accessible to us and, not surprisingly, it will take some time for this experience to mature and stabilize.

Owning the power that lies in our shadow is a particularly challenging task. We can't own it in the sense of possessing it, for the ego is far too small a container and will inflate out of hand. If one were to possess it, one would likely announce that he was God or, equally outlandish, that God was dead. Nietzsche came perilously close to this and paid for it with his sanity. To project this power is to burden another person with superhuman characteristics that are impossible to bear. It remains for our religious life to find a way to come to terms with this great superpersonal power.

I remember a dream of some thirty years ago that announced this dilemma in my own life:

> There is a ring that gives the wearer incredible power. With the ring one can become invisible, transport oneself anywhere instantly, gain power over others. But as time passes one's control of this

power diminishes and it gains control
over the wearer. A young man is running
toward me wearing the ring and completely under its power. He has had the
ring for a long time and can no longer do
his magic tricks of invisibility, and so on.
The police are chasing him to take this
dangerous ring away from him before he
does incalculable harm with it. He cannot evade them any longer since the
magic possibilities of the ring have faded
away and only its dark domination
remains. He comes toward me, tosses
the ring into my hands, and the police
then converge on me. I, as a new owner
of the ring, could call upon all its magic
properties and easily escape the police.
But I know in twenty years I would be in
exactly the same situation as the young
man. I have only five seconds of clarity
before the ring gains power over me and
sends me off into an impenetrable inflation. In that five seconds I raise the ring
high above my head and throw it on the
ground as hard as I can. Just at that
moment the police arrive and we all get
down on our knees to make sure that
none of the ring, not even a fragment,
remains that someone might take to
begin the process all over again. We find
no fragment of the ring but only a gold

coloring in the ground that is the ring
dissipated into the ground. The police
congratulate me and we go off to a pool
nearby to admire some goldfish.

This drama is about an ordinary human
being deciding to put the great superpersonal
power back into the earth and not affix it to
his own personal system. At critical moments
in life it is always possible to sort out what
belongs to one and what does not. There is a
moment of sanity when decision is possible. If
one misses that moment, he will probably be
so intoxicated with new power that he will
misuse it.

It is the same when we are dealing with
the power of romantic love. In marriages, too,
we can only hold the ring for a few brief seconds, or we will be destroyed by the 10,000-
volt shock when we see divinity in our mates.
This experience is not something ordinary
humans can endure for long. And so we must
remember to give this energy back to God and
to the earth again. If we can behold the sacred
power in a marriage, then ease back to ordinary voltage, our story will not have to end
like Tristan and Iseult's.

There is another very old tale that warns

us that we must stop and honor the divine as the source of all relationship. This one comes to us from ancient Greece. It is the story of Atalanta, a strong and intelligent woman who happened to be the fastest runner in the land. She went with Jason to find the Golden Fleece and even wrestled with the men. When pressed to marry, she said that she would only accept a suitor who could beat her in a footrace, knowing this was an impossible task. Atalanta is very much like our modern heroines—ambitious and accomplished, and comfortable in the world of men. The trouble is, she has no training in the art of relationship.

One day the youth Hippomenes fell in love with her and begged the goddess Aphrodite for her aid. Intrigued by this maiden who cared so little for her beauty, Aphrodite gave the suitor three golden apples and during the race, Hippomenes rolled them at her feet. When Atalanta stopped to pick them up, the young man took the lead and won her as his bride. But, alas, the eager lovers went off to consummate their marriage without making a sacrifice at the temple of Aphrodite. The goddess was so enraged that she changed them into lions and made them pull her chariot across the sky.

The ancient world had no illusions about romance; they knew that these feelings came, fleetingly, as a gift from the gods. There was less inflation here: humans were only carriers of divine energy. Today when this energy is bestowed on us, we need a ritual of thanksgiving to contain it, and a way of returning it to its rightful source.

Paradox as Religious Experience

When we consciously approach the shadow, we examine a very powerful aspect of our personality that is almost universally shunned and avoided. And in this way, we enter the realm of paradox.

Paradox is that artesian well of meaning we need so badly in our modern world. All the great myths give instructions on this subject and remind us that the treasure will be found in one of the least likely or popular places. What good could come from Nazareth? What of value could be buried in your own backyard? In the inner life, what good could come from your own shadow? Strangely, the best can come from this neglected quarter. We will go to almost any length to avoid this painful paradox; but in that refusal we only confine ourselves to the useless experience of contradiction. Contradiction brings the crushing burden of meaninglessness. One can endure any suffering if it has meaning; but meaninglessness is unbearable. Contradiction is barren and destructive, yet paradox is creative. It is a powerful embracing of reality. All religious experience in its historical form is expressed in paradox; observe the Christian creeds that have been formulated in such paradoxical language. While contradiction is static and unproductive, paradox makes room for grace and mystery.

Example: Every human experience can be expressed in terms of paradox. The electric plug in the wall has two prongs, access to a positive and negative electrical charge. From this opposition comes the usefulness of the electric current. Day is comprehensible only in contrast to night. Masculinity has relevance only in contrast to femininity. Activity has meaning only in relation to rest. Taste is a matter of contrasts. Up is only possible in the presence of down. What would north be without south? Where would I be without you? Where is joy not bounded by sobriety?

For some incomprehensible reason we often refuse this paradoxical nature of reality and, in an idiot moment, think we can function outside it. The very moment we do this, we translate paradox into opposition. When leisure is torn loose from work, both are spoiled. Personal suffering begins when we are crucified between these opposites. If we try to embrace one without paying tribute to the other, we degrade paradox into contradiction. Yet both pairs of opposites must be equally honored. To suffer one's confusion is the first step in healing.* Then the pain of contradiction is transformed into the mystery of paradox.

The quickest way I know to break a person is to give him or her two sets of contradicting values—which is exactly what we do, in modern culture, with our Sunday and Monday moralities. We are taught by Christianity to follow a set of values that are almost entirely disregarded in everyday business life. How is a person to cope?

At some point—usually in midlife—the

---

*It is instructive that the word *suffer* comes from the Latin *sub plus ferre*, meaning to bear or to allow.

tension becomes too great and these two opposing points of view demand a new and different treatment. We can no longer allow ourselves to be torn between the two. The pressure becomes so great that something has to give.

We hate paradox since it is so painful getting there, but it is a very direct experience of a reality beyond our usual frame of reference and yields some of the greatest insights. It forces us beyond ourselves and destroys naive and inadequate adaptations. Most of the time, we support two warring points of view and evade the confrontation. This is the character of many modern lives. In an ordinary day we have endless examples of this divided opinion. I need to go to work but I don't want to; I don't like my neighbor but I have to be civil with him; I should lose some weight but I like certain foods so much; my budget is overtaxed but . . . These are the contradictions that we live with constantly. Yet these illusions should be disillusioned, painful as this may be. We cannot simply blot out one side of the balance. But we can change our way of looking at the problem. If we accept these opposing elements and endure the collision of them in full consciousness, we embrace the paradox. The capacity for paradox is the measure of spiritual strength and the surest sign of maturity.

To advance from opposition (always a quarrel) to paradox (always holy) is to make a leap of consciousness. That leap takes us through the chaos of middle age and gives a vista that enlightens the remaining years of life.

It is a valuable exercise to list the oppositions that we face, then try to restore them to the realm of paradox. We can start with these two sets of values: the everyday practical attitudes that nearly everyone agrees to and the religious instruction that we are given.

Practical Values	Religious Values
Winning	Losing
Income	Outgo
Eating	Fasting
Action	Passivity
Earning	Giving
Owning	Selling all and giving to the poor
Possession	Poverty
Activity	Repose
Sex	Celibacy
Decisiveness	Observation

Freedom	Obedience to authority
Choice	Duty
Democracy	Obedience
Sharp consciousness	Meditative consciousness
Sobriety	Ecstasy
Focus	Vision
Belief that more is better	Belief that less is better

Few people would argue with the practical values just listed. To win is good; to receive is on the plus side of the scale; a good income is excellent; to eat is life itself; action gets things done; to earn is the badge of responsibility; to own is to be a pillar of the community and a person of substance; possession is security; to be busy is a virtue (the devil finds work for idle hands); sex is the cornerstone of our lives; to be decisive is to be productive and reliable; freedom is the mainspring of our form of government; choice is sacrosanct for free people; power means effectiveness; focused consciousness is the best antidote to the dreamy half-awakeness of primitive people; clarity is important; everyone knows that more is better.

These virtues are blue-chip and beyond controversy in our Western society. Our culture is based on them and has produced its best works by virtue of them.

But what of the other list, the religious values? We hear of them nearly every Sunday and they are an undertone in our Christian culture. We are told from the pulpit that it is better to give than to receive; sell all thou hast and give to the poor; to fast is to gain spiritual virtue; turn the other cheek; "blessed are the poor in spirit for they shall see God"; "they owned nothing but held all in common." In the story of industrious Martha and quiet Mary, we know that Mary was the better of the two. Celibacy is the highest estate and is prescribed for priest and monk, who are the models of our Christian culture. We're also told: judge not; refer every question to authority; choice should be left to one's superiors; obedience is the greatest virtue; where there is power, there is not love; to be a little dreamy by fasting or exhaustion is to invite a vision; ecstasy is the birthright of every Christian; to be exulted by the wine of Christ is the goal of life.

What a contradiction! Yet every one of us lives in this contradiction whether we consciously adhere to Christian virtues or not. It is built into our language, customs, stories. Our Constitution is based on freedom and democracy—the right to choose one's own way—but our religious teaching has us subservient to something greater than our private selves. Here we are directed by the will of God. The contradiction is perhaps no more apparent than in our coins, which bear the phrase "In God We Trust." No wonder there is a movement afoot to delete the phrase since most people no longer trust in God!

I came back from one of my India journeys filled with the religious attitude of that mystical land and meditating on the Hindu and Buddhist way of no-choice. I had been taught by these doctrines that the will of God is always singular and if you think there is a choice between any two alternatives you have not yet done your homework. When the issues are clear, it is absolutely apparent what one should do; there is no choice, for the mind of God is unified and knows no duality.

I was digesting this teaching as I opened a letter from a friend. The masthead of his organization announced, "We Are Dedicated to Making the Field of Choice as Broad as Possible for Every Person." East speaks to

West over a very wide chasm! I had to observe that my Indian friends live in relative peace while my American friends, so devoted to decision making, are a tense and anxious people.

Every single virtue in this world is made valid by its opposite. Light would mean nothing without dark, masculine without feminine, care without abandon. Truths always come in pairs and one has to endure this to accord with reality. To suffer means to allow; and in this sense one suffers the mystery of duality. Whenever you do *this*, something immediately does *that*. Such is reality.

So what now? What do we do with this apparently insufferable contradiction? That is essentially the question that is at the base of every neurotic dissociation and every psychological problem. If we go at the question wrongly we are bound in a neurotic paralysis in which we can do nothing. Then we find we are so anxious that we cannot even do that! We cannot act or be still. This is where many people stand and their suffering is intense. If we begin to do *this*, we are guilt-stricken in the presence of *that*—and we are caught in the endless suffering from which there is no escape. If we do something we enjoy, we spoil it with guilt about what we ought to be doing. If we do what we ought, what we wish for and fantasize about spoils our discipline. Beethoven wrote of this in musical language in the scherzo of his Ninth Symphony. The music goes round and round and round and there's no resolution. The final movement does find a release, a synthesis, and it ends with a great shout of joy.

Did your high school mathematics teacher ever trick you (as an educational device) by proving to you that 2 equals 3? There is the proof on the blackboard and no student is quick enough to catch the error. The trick is that something was divided by 0 along the way and since this is impossible it gives a false result. We set up our psychological equations in much this same manner and get an equally false solution.

There is a fundamental error in the oppositions I have been laying out. Duality is as false as the proof that 2 equals 3. If this were the true reality, I don't think anyone could survive. Our psychological structures would collapse. And sometimes they do!

Our error (thank God there is an error or life would be unendurable!) is that we use the word *religious* in a wrong way. The word *religion* stems from the Latin roots *re*, meaning again, and *ligare*, meaning to bind, bond, or bridge. Our common word *ligature* comes from the same root. Religion means, then, to bind together again. It can never be affixed to one of a pair of opposites. In the preceding discussion I have pointed out the secular versus the religious attitude. This is a flaming, flagrant error and is the seat of most of the neurotic suffering in humankind. To think that one way of action is profane and another sacred is to make terrible misuse of the language. There is no such thing as a religious act or list of characteristics. There can only be a religious insight that bridges or heals. This is what restores and reconciles the opposites that have been torturing each of us. The religious faculty is the art of taking the opposites and binding them back together again, surmounting the split that has been causing so much suffering. It helps us move from contradiction—that painful condition where things oppose each other—to the realm of paradox, where we are able to entertain simultaneously two contradictory notions and give them equal dignity. Then, and only then, is there the possibility of grace, the spiritual experience of contradictions brought into a coherent whole—giving us a unity greater than either one of them.

To say that it is better to give than to receive is to indulge in the same kind of error that proves that 2 equals 3. To focus on one of a pair of opposites as "religious" is truly a mistake. It is only the realm of synthesis that is worthy of the adjective.

We must restore the word *religious* to its true meaning; then it will regain its healing power. To heal, to bond, to join, to bridge, to put back together again—these are our sacred faculties.

The Miracle of Paradox

To transfer our energy from opposition to paradox is a very large leap in evolution. To engage in opposition is to be ground to bits by the insolubility of life's problems and events. Most people spend their life energy supporting this warfare within themselves. One has only to listen to any candid conversation among friends to hear a recital of all the things that are going wrong for them. A huge amount of energy is wasted by modern people in opposing their own situation. Opposition is something like a short circuit; it also drains our energy away like a hemorrhage.

To transform opposition into paradox is to allow both sides of an issue, both pairs of opposites, to exist in equal dignity and worth. Example: I should be working at my project this morning but I don't feel like it and want to do something else. These two opposing wishes will cancel each other if I let them remain in opposition. But if I sit with them awhile they will fashion a solution that is agreeable to both; or even better, a situation that is superior to either one. Sometimes a compromise may present itself that is better than opposition but is still not a good solution. I may take the dog for a walk and then settle down to some work, trying to accommodate both my need for industry and my need for play. But this is not true paradox. If I can stay with my conflicting impulses long enough, the two opposing forces will teach each other something and produce an insight that serves them both. This is not compromise but a depth of understanding that puts my life in perspective and allows me to know with certainty what I should do. That certainty is one of the most precious qualities known to humankind.

I am tempted to describe such a solution, but that would be misleading since every such solution has to grow from the unique situation that one faces. Formulas or devices are never enough at such a moment. The solution must rise from the dynamics of the opposing energies that are facing each other.

Isak Dinesen, the Danish author of *Out of Africa,* once wrote that there are three occasions for true happiness in human beings. The first is a surplus of energy. The second is the cessation of pain. The third is the absolute certainty that one is doing the will of God. The first is the province of youth. The second lasts only for a brief moment. The third is to be won by virtue of much work— inner work. If one has progressed past the duality of life, one has come to the absolute certainty that one is doing the will of God. This is the joy that every one of us knows to be our true heritage and that haunts us or inspires us as the goal of life.

This requires nothing less than taking our two lists of virtues and instead of entering a neurotic struggle that pits one against the other, allowing them the noble status of paradox. It is good to win; it is also good to lose. It is good to have; it is also good to give to the poor. Freedom is good; so is the acceptance of authority. To view the elements of our life in this paradoxical manner is to open up a whole new series of possibilities. Let us not say that the opposites are antithetical but that they make up a divine reality that is accessible to us in our human condition. It is wrong to say that one of a pair is secular and the other religious. We must retrain ourselves to think that each represents a divine truth. It is only our inability to see the hidden unity that is problematic. To stay loyal to paradox is to *earn the right to unity.* Indeed, the most valuable experience of the Christian life is the unitive vision, that most treasured experience of mystical theology, which is won by surrendering to paradox. The medieval world understood this experience, which took one beyond the collision of opposites and brought one into harmony with God.

If we stay with the paradox we will find that single eye that is beyond a quarrel and a compromise. We will find instead a unified attitude that marshals all our energy to a

fine focus. This is worthy of the term enlightenment.

The Paradox of Love and Power

Probably the most troublesome pair of opposites to reconcile is love and power. Our modern world is torn to shreds by this dichotomy
and one finds many more failures than successes in the attempt to reconcile them.

It is not possible to live a human life without both of these elements. Power without
love becomes brutal; love without power is
insipid and weak. Yet when two people get
close to each other, there is generally an
explosion in their lives. Most of the recrimina-
tion between quarreling lovers or spouses
involves the collision of power and love. To
give each its due and endure the paradoxical
tension is the noblest of all tasks. It is only
too easy to embrace one at the expense of the
other; but this precludes the synthesis that is
the only real answer. Failure invites a breaking apart—divorce, disunion, quarrel. A true
paradox makes for a strong devotion and a
mystical union powerful enough to endure the
problems.

Fanaticism is always a sign that one has adopted one of a pair of opposites at the expense of the other. The high energy of fanaticism is a frantic effort to keep one half of the truth at bay while the other half takes control. This always yields a brittle and unrelatable personality. This kind of righteousness depends on "being right." We may want to hear what the other is saying, but be afraid when the balance of power starts to shift. The old equation is collapsing and you are sure that you will lose yourself if you "give in." And how the ego works to keep the status quo! In this event, one must put some faith in transcendence—and have the courage to sacrifice a point of view for the sake of the relationship.

Ligare, the heart of the religious experience, is to bond, repair, draw together, to make whole, to find that which is anterior to the split condition. Our future lies in this religious vision.

The Shadow as Entree to Paradox

We began with a discussion of the shadow and we may well ask the question, What has paradox to do with the shadow? It has everything to do with the shadow, for there can be no

paradox—that sublime place of reconciliation—until one has owned one's own shadow
and drawn it up to a place of dignity and
worth. To own one's own shadow is to prepare
the ground for spiritual experience. Scripture
and many stories tell us that the stuff of holiness is to be found in the most common
places and events. This is a mythic statement
that the pearl of great price is to be found in
our everyday conflicts and tensions. No one is
lacking in such experiences. Someone once
said that Shakespeare could take the roof off
any house and find an immortal drama. Take
the roof off any human life and one will find
the paradoxes that are the preparation for a
religious life, a vision of that which is greater
than the personal. Conflict to paradox to revelation; that is the divine progression.

Who has not fallen in love with someone
where he or she shouldn't? To keep faith with
this and with one's ethical and moral sense at
the same time is to set the stage for the Self,
something greater than one's self.

Who does not spend much of his time
debating whether to do the disciplined task or
to goof off a bit longer and stay in dreamy
"nowhere"? Neither is holy; but exactly in the
paradox between them lies the holy place.

People come to the consulting room and lay out a collision of values with great embarrassment and agony. They want resolution but would have something even greater if they could ask for the consciousness to bear the paradox. A friend went to her hour with Dr. Meyer in Zurich who was famous for commenting with the single word "ja" to anything he was told. In good English style my friend bravely laid out the complexity of her life. She burst into tears and cried out that she could stand it no longer. "Ja, güt," replied Dr. Meyer. "Now something will happen." This is stark medicine but it is correct for one who has the strength to bear it.

When the unstoppable bullet hits the impenetrable wall, we find the religious experience. It is precisely here that one will grow. Jung once said, "Find out what a person fears most and that is where he will develop next." The ego is fashioned like the metal between the hammer and the anvil.

This is for the brave and one does not easily find a moral or ethical nature strong enough for the process. Heroism could be redefined for our time as the ability to stand paradox.

So, in practicality, what do you do? Just to ask that question takes you off center, for it makes you choose between doing and being. No glib solution will work. An early issue of *Psychology Today* shouted in bold letters on its cover, "Don't Just Do Something. Stand There." Joking as this seems, this is Buddhism brought to our attention at a point where we badly need it. Paradox is brought to its next stage of development by a highly conscious waiting. The ego can do no more; it must wait for that which is greater than itself.

Dr. Marie-Louise von Franz puts it in her straightforward language:

> Jung has said that to be in a situation where there is no way out, or to be in a conflict where there is no solution, is the classical beginning of the process of individuation. It is meant to be a situation without solution: the unconscious wants the hopeless conflict in order to put ego-consciousness up against the wall, so that the man has to realize that whatever he does is wrong, whichever way he decides will be wrong. This is meant to knock out the superiority of the ego, which always acts from the illusion that it has the responsibility of decision. Naturally, if a man says, "Oh well, then I shall just let everything go and make no decision, but just protract and wriggle out of [it]," the whole thing is equally

wrong, for then naturally nothing happens. But if he is ethical enough to suffer to the core of his personality, then generally . . . the Self manifests. In religious language you could say that the situation without issue is meant to force the man to rely on an act of God. In psychological language the situation without issue, which the anima arranges with great skill in a man's life, is meant to drive him into a condition in which he is capable of experiencing the Self. When thinking of the anima as the soul guide, we are apt to think of Beatrice leading Dante up to Paradise, but we should not forget that he experienced that only after he had gone through Hell. Normally, the anima does not take a man by the hand and lead him right up to Paradise; she puts him first into a hot cauldron where he is nicely roasted for a while.*

To consent to paradox is to consent to suffering that which is greater than the ego. The religious experience lies exactly at that point of insolubility where we feel we can proceed no further. This is an invitation to that which is greater than one's self.

---

*Marie-Louise von Franz, *Interpretation of Fairy Tales* (New York: Spring Publications, 1970), sec. VI, p. 4.

3

The Mandorla

Thank God, there is a concept to rescue us from the usual impasse. Happily, we have it in our own Christian culture and do not have to go to exotic places for a solution.

This is the mandorla, an idea from medieval Christianity that is all but unknown today. You will find it in any book on medieval theology but one rarely finds it talked about at present. It is far too valuable a concept to have lost.

Everyone knows what a mandala is, even though *mandala* is a Sanskrit term borrowed from India and Tibet. A mandala is a holy circle or bounded place that is a representation of wholeness. We often find this image in the Tibetan *tanka,* a picture, generally of the Buddha with his many attributes, that hangs on the wall of a prayer room or temple as a reminder of the wholeness of life. Mandalas are devices that remind us of our unity with God and with all living things. In Tibet a teacher often draws a mandala for his student and leaves him to meditate on this symbol for many years before he gives the next step of instruction. The mandala is also found in the rose window in Gothic architecture, and it appears frequently as a healing symbol in Christian art. Mandalas turn up in dreams when the personality is especially fragmented and the dreamer needs this calming symbol. During a particularly taxing time in his life, Dr. Jung drew a mandala every morning to keep his sense of balance and proportion.

The mandorla also has a healing effect, but its form is somewhat different. A mandorla is that almond-shaped segment that is made when two circles partly overlap. It is not by chance that *mandorla* is also the Italian word for almond. This symbol signifies nothing less than the overlap of the opposites that we have been investigating. Generally, the mandorla is described as the overlap of heaven and earth. There is not one of us who is not torn by the competing demands of heaven and earth; the mandorla instructs us how to engage in reconciliation. Christ and the Virgin are often portrayed within the framework of the mandorla. This reminds us that we partake of the nature of both heaven and earth. Christianity makes a wonderful affirmation of the feminine element of life by giving it a place in the mandorla, and the Virgin sits in majesty in the mandorla as often as Christ. The finest examples of the mandorla appear in the west portals of many of the great cathedrals in Europe, with Christ or the Virgin framed this way.

The Healing Nature of the Mandorla

The mandorla is so important for our torn world that we will explore it in detail. We have been talking about pairs of opposites in our examination of the shadow. It has been the nature of our cultural life to set a good possibility against a bad one and banish the bad one so thoroughly that we lose track of its

Mandorla. The Chalice Well, Glastonbury, Somerset, England. Courtesy of Thames & Hudson. Photograph by Reece Winstone.

Mandala. Bhutan wall painting. Photograph by Tom Braise.

existence. These banished elements make up our shadow, but they will not stay in exile forever, and about midlife they come back like Old Testament scapegoats returning from the desert.

What can one do when the banished elements demand a day of reckoning? Then it is time for an understanding of the mandorla.

The mandorla has a wonderfully healing and encouraging function. When one is tired or discouraged or so battered by life that one can no longer live in the tension of the opposites, the mandorla shows what one may do. When the most herculean efforts and the finest discipline no longer keep the painful contradictions of life at bay, we are all in need of the mandorla. It helps us transfer from a cultural life to a religious life. (Fortunately, this does not end our cultural life, for by now it is well enough established to survive on its own.)

The mandorla begins the healing of the split. The overlap generally is very tiny at first, only a sliver of a new moon; but it is a beginning. As time passes, the greater the overlap, the greater and more complete is the healing. The mandorla binds together that which was torn apart and made unwhole—unholy. It is the most profound religious experience we can have in life.

The mandorla is the place of poetry. It is the duty of a true poet to take the fragmented world that we find ourselves in and to make unity of it. In the *Four Quartets*, T. S. Eliot writes, "The fire and the rose are one."* By overlapping the two elements of fire and a flower, he makes a mandorla. We are pleased to the depth of our soul to be told that the fire of transformation and the flower of rebirth are one and the same. All poetry is based upon the assertion that *this* is *that*. When the images overlap, we have a mystical statement of unity. We feel there is safety and sureness in our fractured world, and the poet has given us the gift of synthesis.

Great poetry makes these leaps and unites the beauty and the terror of existence. It has the ability to surprise and shock—to remind us that there are links between the things we have always thought of as opposites.

---

*T. S. Eliot, *Four Quartets*, in *The Complete Poems and Plays: 1909–1950* (New York: Harcourt Brace, 1971), p. 145.

Language as Mandorla

All language is a mandorla; a well-structured sentence is of this nature. That is probably why we like to talk so much; good talk restores unity to a fragmented world. A badly formed sentence with poor grammatical structure offends us—probably because it overlaps elements poorly and fails in its unifying task.

Our principal verb *to be* is the great unifier. A sentence with the verb *to be* is a statement of identity and heals the split between two elements. This is honored by observing the subjective form for the predicate of the verb *to be*. We say, "I am he," not "I am him." I and he are the same, a statement of the mystical union of diversity.

All sentences make identity even apart from the verb *to be*, though it may be less obvious. Every verb makes holy ground. "I will go home" or "I will play music now" imply a special identity to "I" and "home" or "I" and "music." To make any well formed sentence is to make unity out of duality. This is immensely healing and restorative. We are all poets and healers when we use language correctly. One makes a mandorla every time one says something that is true.

A sentence is something like a mathematical equation with the verb representing the equal sign. A correct sentence says that the subject equals the object and annuls the quarrel between the two. The split inherent in duality is healed.

Languages rich in verbs are more powerful than those relying mostly on nouns. Chinese and Hebrew are the former. Human speech is more effective if it relies mainly on verbs. If you build mainly on nouns it will be weak; if you rely on adjectives and adverbs you have lost your way. The verb is holy ground, the place of the mandorla. One can examine the great speeches of Shakespeare to find the nobility and the healing power of strong verbs.

A friend sent me a tape recorder long before they were in common use. Instructions were noted: "Plug this in, press button A, listen to the tape on the machine. Then turn the tape over, press button B, and make a tape in reply." For a minute or two when I began my taped response, I was awkward; I couldn't think of anything to say. Yet when the tape ran out an hour later I was angry, for I had not nearly exhausted all I wanted to express. Thus began a tape correspondence that was extremely valuable to me. When I was distressed, I would make a tape and find that I had often talked my way through a dilemma. I did what Freud called "the talking cure," for language, properly used, is a highly curative agency. My friend lives far away and we meet infrequently. At one rare meeting my friend said, "Robert, why is it that you are so much more intelligent on tape than in conversation? Don't answer; I know. On the tape I don't interrupt!" Talking to him by tape had engaged my feeling function and given me the freedom to process my own thoughts. You can give another person a precious gift if you will allow him to talk without contaminating his speech with your own material. Given the right container, we can make mandorlas of speech and cure many things. We become poets in our own right in the proper circumstances.

It is a miracle to listen to someone (even oneself) say, "Perhaps this, perhaps that, maybe, it follows that, I wonder if"—all like a dog chasing its tail. But gradually, the two disparate circles begin to overlap and the mandorla grows. This is healing. This is ligature, the essence of religious experience.

All good stories are mandorlas. They speak of *this* and *that* and gradually, through the miracle of story, demonstrate that the opposites overlap and are finally the same. We like to think that a story is based on the triumph of good over evil; but the deeper truth is that good and evil are superseded and the two become one. Since our capacity for synthesis is limited, many stories can only hint at this unity. But any unity, even a hint, is healing.

Do you remember the story of Moses and the burning bush? There are many bushes and much burning; but in *this* story the bush and the burning overlap; the bush is not consumed and we know that two orders of reality have been superimposed. In a moment we find that God is near—the result of the overlap.

Whenever you have a clash of opposites in your being and neither will give way to the other (the bush will not be consumed and the fire will not stop), you can be certain that God is present. We dislike this experience intensely and avoid it at any cost; but if we can endure it, the conflict-without-resolution is a direct experience of God.

A mandorla is a prototype of conflict resolution. It is the art of healing, if you will.

Shakespeare wrote of his art:

> The poet's eye, in a fine frenzy rolling,
> Doth glance from heaven to earth, from
>   earth to heaven;
> And as imagination bodies forth
> The forms of things unknown, the poet's
>   pen
> Turns them to shapes and gives to airy
>   nothing
> A local habitation and a name.*

Here Shakespeare is reconciling heaven and earth and giving a place and a name to the human faculties that can cope with this wide vision.

To reconcile so great a span as heaven and earth is beyond our ordinary way of seeing; generally, two irreconcilable opposites (guilt and need) make neurotic structures in us. It takes a poet—or the poet in us—to overlap such a pair and make a sublime whole of them. Who but Shakespeare could bring the airy nothing of heaven into consonance with the heavy reality of earth and give it a form

---

*William Shakespeare, *A Midsummer Night's Dream*, act 5, scene 1, lines 12–17, in *The Riverside Shakespeare* (Boston: Houghton Mifflin, 1974).

that ordinary humans can understand? Who but the Shakespeare in yourself?

Take *this* and take *that*—and make a mandorla of them.

In your own poetic struggles you may make only the tiniest sliver of a mandorla that will vanish a few minutes later. Where is the inspiration of yesterday that was so thrilling? But if you repeat this often enough it will become the permanent base of your functioning. It can be hoped that by the end of your life the two circles will be entirely overlapped. When one is truly a citizen of both worlds, heaven and earth are no longer antagonistic to each other. Finally one sees that there was only one circle all the time. This is the true fulfillment of the Christian goal, the beatific vision so prized in medieval theology. The two circles were only the optical illusion of our capacity—and need—to see things double.

Mandorla making is not confined to verbal form. An artist makes a mandorla with form, color, visual tension. A musician does the same with rhythm, form, and tone.

Since music is a developed faculty in me, I am aware of the mandorla in this mode more than any other. There is a wonderful moment

about three-quarters of the way through
Bach's *St. Matthew Passion*. The scene is the
crucifixion and an alto is singing the solo
"Lord Jesus Stretches Forth His Hand." The
alto voice weaves its serene vocal line while a
contra fagotto, a particularly rough instru-
ment in the lower register, makes a series of
leaps of the natural seventh. This interval (an
octave minus one note) is forbidden in classi-
cal counterpoint since it resembles the bray-
ing of a donkey to a startling degree. Ferde
Grofé makes dramatic use of this in his
Grand Canyon Suite to portray donkeys going
down the canyon trails.* But Bach, in his
genius, weaves these two elements together—
the most serene and the most ragged and disjointed—and makes a mandorla of it. The
serene alto voice goes its tranquil way while
the contra fagotto makes a grotesque buffoon-
ery of the natural seventh leap in the bass
line. The two together make a sublime whole.
It is one of the most healing experiences in
the world for me to listen to this moment of

---

*A friend of mine turned his counterpoint lesson in to a
distinguished teacher who returned it marked in red pencil,
"The leap of a natural seventh is reserved for donkeys!!" My
friend returned the paper with the addition, "And Bach!" He
was dismissed from the school.

genius. If these two extremes can be woven together to make a masterpiece, perhaps I can bring the ragged, disjointed elements of my own life together.

A particularly powerful form of mandorla can be seen in the customs of South American *curanderos*, who are a curious mixture of primitive shaman and Catholic priest. Their *mesa* (table) is an altar where they say Mass for the healing of their patients. They divide this altar into three distinct sections. The right is made up of inspiring elements such as a statue of a saint, a flower, a magic talisman; the left contains very dark and forbidding elements such as weapons, knives, or other instruments of destruction. The space between these two opposing elements is a place of healing. The message is unmistakable; our own healing proceeds from that overlap of what we call good and evil, light and dark. It is not that the light element alone does the healing; the place where light and dark begin to touch is where miracles arise. This middle place is a mandorla.*

------

*I am indebted to Dr. Douglas Sharon, curator of the Museum of Man, Balboa Park, San Diego, California, for this insight.

A mandorla can also be danced. I remember one woman who danced out the conflicting elements in her psyche in her analytical hour. She would portray one part of her life, then move to the opposite side of the room to portray another. This is not familiar ground for me and I was cowering behind my chair by the end of the hour. When finished, she would invite me out of hiding and explain to me what she had been saying in body language.

The criticism may be made that the mandorla is only a private experience and totally divorced from practicality. But the I Ching, in hexagram #61, says, "If a wise man abides in his room his thoughts are heard for more than a thousand miles." If one makes mandorla in the privacy of his interior life, it is heard for more than a thousand miles.

If you find a person who is particularly peaceful or has a healing presence around her, it is probably because she has done her mandorla work. If you want to affect your environment, don't get lost in your activism. Stop for a moment and make a mandorla. Don't just do—*be* something.

People often asked Dr. Jung, "Will we make it?" referring to the cataclysm of our time. He always replied, "If enough people will do their inner work." This soul work is the one thing that will pull us through any emergency. The mandorla is peace-making.

I think the loveliest lines in our Scripture are, "If thy eye be single, thy whole body shall be filled with light" (Matt. 6:22). The right eye sees *this*, the left eye sees *that;* but if one comes to the third eye, the single eye, all will be filled with light. Indian people put a spot of rouge in the center of the forehead to indicate that they are enlightened (or on the way to enlightenment). In the system of chakras that is the highest point attainable by human consciousness. One more chakra, the seventh, exists, but that is beyond our ordinary ability to experience.

Encouraged by Christian practice, most Westerners invest the energy that might go into a mandorla in useless guilt. Guilt is a total waste of time and energy. I used to tease my Baptist grandmother, telling her guilt was a sin. She would get very angry since I was depriving her of her favorite pastime. She thought she was not doing her duty to Jesus if she were not wringing her hands in guilt at her (or my) sinful condition. Guilt creates

nothing; conscious work constructs a mandorla and is healing. The mandorla has no
place for remorse. It asks conscious work of
us, not self-indulgence.

Guilt is also a cheap substitute for paradox. The energy consumed by guilt would be
far better invested in the courageous act of
looking at two sets of truths that have collided
in our personality. Guilt is also arrogant
because it means we have taken sides in an
issue and are sure that we are right. While
this one-sidedness may be part of the cultural
process, it is severely detrimental to the religious life. To lose the power of confrontation
is to lose one's chance at unity—and to miss
the healing power of the mandorla.

It is good to remember that the old symbol
for Christ—the two lines indicating a stylized
fish—is a mandorla. By definition, Christ himself is the intersection of the divine and the
human. He is the prototype for the reconciliation of opposites and our guide out of the
realm of conflict and duality. Early Christians
would make themselves known to one another
in this way: upon meeting, one would scratch
a small circle in the dust. The other would
make a second circle that was slightly overlapping—thus completing a mandorla. This way

of greeting—at a time when Christians were severely persecuted—was powerful and eloquent. It also has meaning for us today. If one has a statement to make, it is good to invite another statement—generally one coming from the shadow—and thus make a mandorla that is greater than either point of view alone.

I remember in high school debating class, our teacher once made us change our positions one minute before the debate. I was in a panic for a moment, then felt the flood of energy that came from getting the overview in a new and different way. Indeed, this experience was so powerful that I won the debate. I think I have won (or superseded) some very serious spiritual debates in my inner life by giving credence to both sides, until a superior point of view could be achieved.

The Human Dimensions of the Mandorla

One can view a human life as a mandorla and as the ground upon which the opposites find their reconciliation. In this way every human being is a redeemer, and Christ is the prototype for this human task. Every glance between a man and a woman is also a mandorla, a place where the great opposites of masculinity and femininity meet and honor one another. The mandorla is the divine container in which a new creation begins to form and germinate. Scripture never tires of speaking about courtship and marriage as the symbol for our reconciliation with the spirit. Toni Sussman, a Jungian analyst in London and one of my early teachers, once told me that sex is the one symbol in dreams that is always creative. Even if it occurs in violent form in a dream, still, it is speaking to us of reconciliation and creation. Such is the high place of union in the symbolic world. (This is always true inwardly but cannot be presumed outwardly.)

If we have a powerful mandorla experience (and what a joy it is!), we can be sure it will be brief. We must then return to the world of dualities, of time and space, to continue our ordinary life. The shadow is created all over again, and a new experience of transformation is required. The great individuals in history have only momentary glimpses of wholeness and they, too, return very quickly to the world of ego-shadow confrontation. There is a Hindu proverb: "Anyone who thinks he is enlightened certainly is not!"

Our human situation divides us over and over again into ego-shadow opposition, no matter where we start. This is probably why St. Augustine said, "To act is to sin." As long as we take our place in society, we will pay for it by bearing a shadow. And society will pay a general price with collective phenomena such as war, violence, and racism. This is why the religious life speaks of another realm, heaven, and of the millennium, as the culmination of the inner life. Culture and religion have different aims.

To balance out our cultural indoctrination, we need to do our shadow work on a daily basis. The first reward for this is that we diminish the shadow we impose on others. We contribute less to the general darkness of the world and do not add to the collective shadow that fuels war and strife. But the second result is that we prepare the way for the mandorla—that high vision of beauty and wholeness that is the great prize of human consciousness.

The ancient alchemists understood this process. In alchemy one goes through four stages of development: the *nigredo*, in which one experiences the darkness and depression

117

of life; the *albedo*, in which one sees the brightness of things; the *rubedo*, where one discovers passion; and finally the *citrino*, where one appreciates the goldenness of life. After all this comes a full-color mandorla. This is the *pavanis*, the peacock's tail that contains all the preceding hues. One cannot stop this process until one has brought it to the *pavanis*, that concert of colors that contains everything.

Wrongly done, the many colors of life produce a grayness, and all the colors neutralize each other into a dull monotony. Correctly done, the *pavanis* comes and all the colors of life make a magnificent and rich pattern. The mandorla is not the place of neutrality or compromise; it is the place of the peacock's tail and rainbows.